MW00462827

Paiges of Wisdom
Sue Paige

Paiges of Wisdom
Copyright © 2015 by Sue Paige

Published by PMA Press
318 Half Day Rd. #319
Buffalo Grove, IL. 60089
847-478-1088

Manufactured in the United States of America.
All rights reserved.

Dedicated with love to my family

To Jeff,
Thank you for the wonderful relationship we shared,
for the years of love, friendship, our children,
and our shared vision. 'Til we meet again, my love…

To my children, Robert, Jennifer, Renee and David,
Thank you for all the lessons you have taught me,
the love we've shared and the life we've created
together. You have been my greatest teachers,
supporters and my motivation throughout my life.
My love for you knows no bounds!

To my grandchildren,
Bobby, Jeffrey, Kaitlyn and Ryan,
You are the joy of my life! So loving and innocent.
There is no love like a grandchild's love!

To those that have walked through the doors of
Pathways, thank you for sharing yourselves with us,
for all the lessons learned and the love we shared,
to us you became family!

*"The best part of life is when your family becomes
your friends, and your friends become your family."*
- Danica Whitfield

Special thanks

I want to give special thanks to everyone that made this book possible, beginning with Stephanie Beeby, who believed in me and encouraged me to do this.

To Kelly Smith, Terri Ungar Coughlin and Lisa Krych for writing down the quotes as they came out of my mouth during classes. Thank you.

To my brother, David Scahill, for taking this book from a dream to reality. Thank you for always being a strong support in my life.

To April Bishop, Chelsea Lamont and Deborah Lieber for your endless support to get this book ready for print and to press. I am so grateful to all of you.

To J Cangialosi and Becky Sonnack for editing. To Bryan Robb and Chelsea Lamont for brainstorming the cover and Tim Mooney for creating the first cover and Stephanie Kelly and Colin Emch-Wei for the second. Thank you!

And to all the grads that have shared their stories bringing about the quotes that you will find in this book, thank you all.

The reason for this book...

The reason for this book is to give to others thoughts that have come out of the seminars we teach that empower people to look within and find the greatness that lives inside each of us.

As we discover this inside ourselves and begin sharing it with the world, our world becomes a better place. And the better we feel about ourselves, the better we treat others!

Each day close your eyes, take a deep breath, and ask yourself what you need to focus on. Open to a page and read it. Focus for that day on what you have read, where you see it showing up for you in your life and what actions you would like to take in order to change it or incorporate it.

*It all begins
and
ends with you!*

1

When we recognize our
own special talents
and uniqueness,
there is no need or desire
to judge another.

*When we are able to recognize and accept our
own gifts and unique talents we begin to see
those in others. We stop comparing ourselves
as better than or less than another and we
then know that there is no need to judge.*

*We start to see the importance and love that we each
bring and begin to understand that judgment comes
from the fear that we are not enough.*

*Look to see what your talents and gifts are.
What is special about you?
See, also, the gifts in others and learn from
those gifts, then we can walk hand in hand
to create something greater than
what we could create alone.*

Live with integrity.
Align your words,
your actions,
and your behaviors ~
with your vision!

When living our life with integrity, everything works better. If our words match our actions it creates trust in all our relationships. Those around us know that we will follow through and do what we say we will do. We begin to trust ourselves and develop an internal strength knowing we can count on ourselves.

We are able to manifest our dreams when our actions are aligned with our vision. We live with honesty, love, openness and vulnerability.

What is one thing you can do today to match your words with your actions?

The greatest gift to
yourself and others
is to live life authentically.

*Living an authentic life is a blessing
to you and to those around you.
A life that is genuine and real has nothing to hide,
no need to impress, no judgment
or fear holding it back.*

*Living authentically gives us freedom to be ourselves
wherever we are, with whomever we choose,
doing whatever we want.*

*Imagine yourself free to be you,
what would you do?
What would you create in the world?*

If you want to be loved, love first;
if you want to be heard, listen first;
if you want to be seen for who you are, see them first;
you must be willing to give the
very thing you most want ~ first!

*Often we wait to feel loved before opening our
hearts and giving our love. If those around us are
not feeling loved and appreciated in their lives,
they do not have the space to give that love to us.
Therefore if we want to be loved we need to love first.
It is the same with being heard or seen.
If we want to be heard we need to
listen to those we love.
They will need to share enough to be
"empty," and only then will they be able to hear us.
When we want others to see our greatness,
we need to be willing to see
the goodness in them first.*

*Who do you need to give love to today?
Show them they are special.
Who do you need to listen to today?
Show them they are important.
Who do you need to see the greatness in today?
Share the greatness you see in them.*

*Become the kind of person
that you want to spend the
rest of your life with!*

As you look for a relationship write down the key characteristics and attributes that you want in a partner. Recognize which of these attributes and characteristics you have not developed, and then become those same attributes and characteristics! As you develop those parts of yourself you will find yourself feeling more complete and whole.

As you become the person you are looking for in a relationship you will find that you are no longer feeling the need to have someone in your life to fill the void, as you are now filling it yourself. Your life will become more joyful and the partner you have been searching for will come along. What a gift you will be to each other!

A heart that touches other
hearts deeply never dies!
It remains alive in those
that are left behind.

As we open our hearts and touch others,
they will remember, and carry in their
hearts what we said or did forever.

The touch from your heart travels from the
people you touch today to those they touch.
They will share the experiences they had
with you that they treasure, they will teach
what you taught them, and touch others
in the way you touched them.

Depending on how deeply you touch them,
you can live on forever.

Fear lives in the past,
and in the future,
but not in the moment!

Come to the moments of life
where joy and love reside!

Each moment we make a choice as to what moment we are going to live in. We are either reminiscing about the past and living in our memories, or we are living in our dreams of the future. Yet in both those places what we experience is fear and we miss what is happening right in this moment in front of us. This robs us of our creativity and joy.

We find that when we can be fully present in the moments of life, they are full of love and incredibly rewarding. We are creative, open, and full of possibilities. We experience what each moment brings to us with childlike wonder and joy. We see the magic that life holds.

Do this simple exercise today to bring yourself into the moment. If you find yourself in the past or present focus on your feet, feel the ground under you and bring yourself to the moment.

Live the life you
have dreamt of,
it will come to life
before your eyes.

Our dreams come to us because we are
meant to bring them into reality.
We have everything we need to make
those dreams concrete.
We often tend to wait for the right
moment, thinking that we need
to do something special in order to
make it happen.
When we believe that we are enough,
and walk with conviction into that dream,
living it each day, our dreams manifest.
What is one thing you can do today to live that dream?

*Children learn by what we do,
not by what we say...
be aware of your actions
as that is what you are
teaching them.*

*We tell our children not to lie, to always tell the
truth, that life works best for those that tell the
truth and are open and honest.*

*The phone rings. It's a salesperson we don't want
to talk to, so we tell our children to tell the person
we are not home or we are predisposed. Subtle
yet powerful. The message the child hears is that it
is ok to lie sometimes. There are so many times
we give our children double messages:
we say one thing, yet do another.*

*Our children watch what we do and mimic that
behavior. If we are afraid and hold back, they see that
and hold themselves back. As they are growing up we
are the ones they watch to know if the world is safe and
how they should act in it. If we are fearful they grow
up thinking that there is something to be afraid of. If
we don't speak up and take care of ourselves, neither
do they. If we hit them or our spouse they grow up
thinking hitting is ok. If we lie sometimes, so do they.*

*Yet, if we are out there going after our goals treating
others with love and respect so are they. Be the person
you want your children to become.*

*Who are you inspiring with
your actions today?*

We often think that our actions do not have much of an impact, yet the reality is that our actions impact others everyday.

If someone was watching how you live your life would they be inspired? What lasting impression would you leave today?

If we are inspired in our lives, taking strides that are outside our comfort zone, and living life to its fullest, we are inspiring those around us. If we are giving with no attachments, we are inspiring. If we are listening and challenging those we love to be the best they can be, we are inspiring.

Who are the people that have inspired you in your life? What have they inspired you to do or to become? Who do you want to INSPIRE today?

What we see in someone else
is only a reflection of ourselves;
be the greatness you see in another.

We can only see in another something that resides within ourselves. Whether it is something we admire about them or have a difficult time with, people around us are constant reflections of ourselves.
If I find myself in judgment of them or angry at their behavior, I need to stop and ask, where or how am I doing that behavior in my life. Often we just want to make them wrong, and that allows us to shut our eyes to our own behavior. You will be amazed at what gifts you will receive for your life by questioning what you need to see and learn.

On the other side of the coin those we are inspired by, see the greatness in, or admire, offer us the same reflection to view. What you see in that person also resides in you, yet you may have been denying that asset in yourself. As you watch those that you admire, look to see where or how you are like them in your life. Begin to own the wonder and greatness that lives within you today.

Make peace with your past
so you don't have to keep
reliving it.

Things that have happened to us in the past make lasting impressions on us. When we examine those things closely we can see that we have made decisions about life that unconsciously drive our decisions and behavior at a deeper level today. The same decisions or behavior happen over and over until we examine them to see what it is we need to know, learn or change.

If you are wondering why you attract certain types of people, or why the same things happen over and over, then it is time to examine the beliefs you have around those things. Once you make peace with them they will no longer continue to show up in your life.

Make peace today, so that you have an even greater tomorrow.

LOOK beyond your limits,
MOVE beyond who you think you are,
FEEL the magnificence of being human,
KNOW you can accomplish anything,
BE your possibilities!

*We often stop at the end of our comfort zone, yet
once we MOVE outside of that, we begin to see
all that we are capable of creating and being.
As we expand our comfort zone we begin to FEEL the
magnificence that resides within us. We FEEL more
alive and excited about what is possible for us. We
begin to KNOW what we are capable of creating, doing
and having. When we are constantly challenging that
comfort zone and taking that next step outside of it,
we begin to BE our possibilities.*

The moment is NOW. Begin today.

*Broken agreements are not
about saying "I'm sorry."
Only your actions can truly say
"I'm sorry."*

How often have you heard someone say, "I'm sorry" yet they continue to do the same behavior over and over, continuing to say I am sorry? Do their words really mean anything, or are they empty promises that are consistently broken?

When you want to truly say you are sorry follow those words up with these three things:

Don't do that action again. Do whatever it takes to change your behavior so that you are not repeating that action.

Come up with a plan with that person as to what you can do differently if it would happen again.

Do a make up. Do something that is only for that person, something that has them feeling special and loved. And most of all, your actions will say you are truly sorry.

Remember your actions speak LOUDER than your words. Show them you are sorry!

If you are willing to do whatever it takes, you will have whatever it is you want.

We are such creative beings, and yet often we try a few things and then give up or quit on our dream or goals when we don't achieve them. The obstacles we come up against when going towards our goals are there to prepare us for the skills we will need when we get what we want. As we overcome those obstacles we gain momentum and strength. We begin to feel more and more confident and excited and that energy can be used to propel us forward.

If you are willing to do whatever it takes with integrity, love and commitment, you will create those dreams of yours.

Reaching out for support in creating those dreams or goals is a huge part of moving through the obstacles that you encounter. When you continue to move forward the DREAM or GOAL is yours. Keep going.

The only thing that stands between
you and what you want from life,
is simply the will to pursue it and
the faith to believe that it is possible.

We are each given dreams to create.
They show up in our heads and when they
do we need to set out on the path of creating those
dreams. Often we let the dreams go due to our fears:
too much going on in our lives at the time, or our
desire and will to attain that dream is overshadowed
by our belief we cannot do it.

If the dream lives within your thoughts,
it is meant for you to create, all you
have to do is pursue it and not give up.
Anything you want to create is possible if you
believe it in your heart and allow yourself
to follow through with your actions.
Begin today.

*If you find yourself going
in the wrong direction,
STOP and choose another direction.*

*We need to listen to our inner voice and follow
the instructions it is giving us.*

*As we go in the direction we are being given, we may
find that the results we are creating are working
great or that things are very difficult.*

*The difficulty that you face may be a message that you
are heading in the wrong direction and need to change
course. It does not mean to give up. Just find
another way to create what it is that you want.*

*Keep moving forward.
Make a shift in the direction you are headed.*

You are a dance step:
unique and wonderful,
you have something special
to teach all of us!

Each person is different, unique and important in the greater picture of life. If we were to look for and recognize the value that each person holds and learn what they have to teach us our world would be such a better place.

Each person is a dance step. Imagine the value you would get if you took the time to learn the step they have to offer you. This would be immeasurable in our lives. When we judge someone we miss the value that they bring to us.

Are you willing to postpone judgment and find the value that each person offers you today?

Holding on to anger
does not support you
in getting what you
want out of life.

What does holding on to anger get you?
Why do you think you would want to hold on to anger?
Often when we hold on to the anger, it suppresses
our energy and creativity, yet we continue to hold
on and allow the anger to drive us rather than
releasing the anger and opening ourselves to
the energy that forgiveness brings.

There is no greater gift we give ourselves than
forgiving. You see the anger we hold against someone
does not hurt them, it harms us. When we forgive and
let go of the anger, we are not saying what someone did
is ok. We are allowing ourselves to release what we
think someone's words or actions said about us.

Your relationships will be different,
when you let go.

We often hold on to our expectations, not sharing what we want or are looking for in our relationships. Unless we are willing to share our desires and wants, the relationship cannot be different.

Let go and share what you know.

Do not try to get the person to be who you want them to be, let go and instead be watchful of the actions that show you who they are.

Let go and see who they are and how they show up in a relationship.

People will not make your life perfect.
They can't.
That is your job.

We want people to act a certain way so that we can be comfortable in our relationship with them. Making sure we are comfortable is not their job; that is our job. When we find ourselves upset by something someone else is saying or doing we need to stop in our tracks and look at ourselves.

When you find yourself triggered by someone take time to look inside and see what is going on for you.

Why do you find yourself reacting? Has this same thing happened to you before somewhere? Is it something you have done in the past?

Love for ourselves starts from the inside ~
not from someone or something
outside of ourselves.

*There is a difference with the love we find inside
ourselves versus the love we find outside of ourselves.
No one can ever take away the love that resides
within us. It is easy to have the love inside of us grow.*

*When we are unconditionally giving, with no thought
of anything in return, our love inside grows...
when we are overcoming our fears, love grows within.
When we are stepping outside our comfort zones and
taking risks, our love grows within. When we are
facing our challenges, our love grows within.*

*When we get love from outside ourselves it feels
wonderful but when that person leaves, as they often
do, we are left empty if we have not built the love
within ourselves. Too often we settle for the love that
comes in the form of approval and validation which
quickly dissipates. Are you looking for love from
inside or outside of yourself?*

Take responsibility for your life;
everything you have in it is because
you choose it.

We choose what we have in our lives either by making the decision to have it or by not making the decision.

We pull things into our lives either consciously or unconsciously to learn from.

There are times that we say we don't want something in our lives and yet we are attracting those exact things in our life.

What are you choosing to have in your life today?

Make a commitment inside yourself
to not waste another moment
of this life.

*We often get wrapped up in doing things that
keep us away from what is most important.*

*If you only had a month to live, what would
you be doing? If you had only one more month
with the people in your life before they were gone,
what would you do with them?*

*The things most people regret in life is what they
did not say or do with someone who was important
to them. Yet we often act as though we have
forever with those we love.*

*The reality is that we can never tell when those people
will be taken from us or when we will be gone.
What special memories do you want to
make with the ones you love?*

What can you do in this moment?

*For as many boulders as you
have carried or created in your life,
you can create that much
greatness in your life!*

*Many of us have had large challenges to overcome
in our lives, yet each of those challenges have
supported us in becoming stronger within ourselves
as we have handled them. That is what
challenges and obstacles in our life are for.
As we overcome them, we become stronger internally
and develop a strong belief in what we are
able to handle and create.*

*As you look at the challenges you have been
handed in life, what strengths do you see
were created while you handled them?*

*Do you find yourself more creative,
more open, more determined?*

*What do you find that you can do now that you
might not have been able to do before?*

When you are too afraid
to let your heart out,
you stay stuck and miss the
people knocking on your
heart saying,
"let me in."

*When we are afraid of getting hurt we close off
our hearts in order to protect them. We become
suspicious and less trusting of others. When we
close up like that there is a higher likelihood of
us getting hurt. We stay stuck in our memories of
old hurts that have not been released, and when we
do that we miss the opportunities of those standing
right in front of us, ready to love us.*

*The reality is that others do NOT hurt us.
Our memories, assumptions and beliefs are what
are hurting us. People's actions are about them,
not us. When we take those actions to say something
about us then we begin to create the pain within
ourselves. At that point we are blinded by our past
memories and beliefs and cannot see the love that
stands in front of us. We put others' faces on that
person. What can you do to let go and forgive those
in your past that have done things that hurt you so
you do not miss the love that is right there?*

Are you ready to let go and be loved?

*You never know when
someone will be taken from you.
Give all your love to the people
in front of you, and you will
live with no regrets.*

How do you want to spend your days? In regret? Feeling love? When we spend our time regretting things we have done or not done we waste time. If you recognize that you have not said or done something, take note, make a commitment to return to do or say what you missed and move on. Otherwise your time is being spent in worry, upset or regret and not in doing those things that are most important to you.

People feel regret for ways they did not show those that they love just how much they love them or how important they are to them. If you find yourself angry or upset with those you love, what will it take you to forgive them so you can move on and spend what time you have left loving them?

If today were the only day you have with them what would you do? How would you spend that time? We often think we have forever with someone rather than treasuring the time we get with them. Treasure today with those you love.

Feel the electricity of life
running through you!
There is nothing like it!

When we take risks in our lives we get the burst of
energy that feels like electricity running through us.
As we overcome our fears and take the challenges that
are standing in front of us we gain value and energy.
Often when we come up against something that we
are afraid to do, we procrastinate or avoid doing it,
and that depresses our energy.

Look at the gifts that are outside your comfort zone
waiting for you! All it takes to have them is to risk and
go outside that comfort zone to attain it. Maybe it is the
girl or guy you would like to ask out, or that job you
would really like to go after. Maybe there is something
you want to say to someone to create more closeness,
or to tell someone that they have upset you.

Take that risk! As you begin walking toward that risk,
watch as the energy grows inside of you. The energy
can be used as excitement to propel you forward or
fear to hold you back, YOU name it.

All it takes, is to go outside that comfort zone and RISK
to attain it. So, choose excitement, overcome those
challenges and go get those dreams.

Who is on your team of life?
Who is supporting you
in creating your dreams?
Be careful to choose those that are
keeping their eyes and hearts open!

It is wonderful to have people in your life that will walk the road to awareness with you. Choose those that will challenge you to move outside your comfort zone, the ones that will tell you what they see in you, the ones that will challenge you when you are complacent and the ones that will hold your hand and celebrate with you as you take those risks. They are the people in your life that will remind you to keep your attention on the goal, support you to see the obstacles and to overcome them!

Choose your team wisely so they will remind you to keep your eyes open and energy up!

Life will always present you with obstacles to overcome. Are you someone that jumps over the hurdles of life, realizing that those hurdles support you in getting stronger? Or are you someone that gives in and wallows in self pity about the hurdles? It is up to you, you are at choice!

As we move through life and toward our goals in life we will always come up against obstacles. The obstacles are there to support us in getting stronger and growing so that when we hit our goal we are able to handle whatever comes from having that goal.

If you look at the things in your life that you have attained and the hurdles you had to overcome in order to get there, you will see how what you learned served you when you got to your goal. Where in your life did you stop when you got to the obstacles and hurdles? What would it take for you to have gotten over those hurdles? What goals do you have in mind now that you want to walk toward?

*Fear and excitement are the same energy.
We name it. We either let that energy propel
us forward or hold us back, it is up to us!*

When we experience fear, it creates a powerful sensation in our bodies. This feeling is there to support us in moving forward with energy in order to face our fears. If you really pay attention, the same energy that you feel when you are really excited about something happens in the same place within your body as the energy you feel with fear.

We name what we are feeling, and allow it to propel us forward or stop us, it is the same energy and we either call it fear or excitement. That feeling is there to say WAKE UP! PAY ATTENTION! SOMETHING IS ABOUT TO HAPPEN. That is all it is saying. What would be different for you if you were to use that feeling to move through those fears with consciousness? What would be different for you?

Our world would be so different if we would just take the time to let others know they are important. If we would look strangers in the eyes and send them love, even if we don't know them.

Your love is important in our world. We can never really tell what is going on for another person from what we see about them. What they have experienced in life makes up who they are and how they see life. The love you have and are willing to show can make such a difference in someone's life.

There is a story about a young man that felt he held no value to those around him, kids didn't want to be his friend, his parents didn't need his support in their lives and basically he felt he had no value. One day he was walking home from school with the intention to kill himself over the weekend. He was carrying all the contents of his locker home so that his family did not have to go through his things after he was dead. He dropped his books and another young man came along and helped him, they began talking and the young man asked him to do something that weekend. They became friends and many years later the young man that helped to pick up the books found out that his friend had planned to kill himself that weekend. His kind actions saved his friend's life.

You really never know whose life you will be saving with a hello, smile, good word, encouragement or praise that you give. We all need to feel important and loved. Share your love today by going out of your way to have those around you feeling important and loved. If we all did that everyday our world would be a different place.

Take a risk each day.
You will be amazed at how you come alive!!
Life takes on new meaning!

If each day we took a step outside our comfort zones and risked, we would find our lives to be exciting and fun. We would continue to gain energy and confidence as well as expand our comfort zones. As you risk it will have you feeling more alive and excited about life. You will feel proud of what you KNOW you can create.

Are you willing to risk to feel great each day?

We each have a responsibility to
show up "in leadership" in our lives.
If we each showed up that way,
what would our world be like?

When I am being real, honest and genuine there is no better way for me to show up for those in my life. I would be giving feedback, honestly supporting them in creating what is important to them.

Unafraid to hold them accountable in a loving way to what they say they want in their lives.

Going beyond my own fears to be there in a supportive way for those I love.

Being an example and inspiration by overcoming your own fears and going after what you want in life is a wonderful way to show those around you that you are there for them as well.

Our actions speak louder than our words.

*By your actions, what have you taken
a stand for in your life?*

People see what we stand for by our actions! The actions a person takes will speak so much louder than their words. If you want to know who a person is, look at their actions. If you want to know what is important to them, look at their actions.

Often people will say they want to be close yet they don't share or spend time with those they say they want to be close to. Have you found yourself in relationships where the person says one thing and does another? If you are listening to their words and hoping for what they say to be true, yet what you see is their actions being different, stop hoping! Look at what is real by looking to their actions, the actions will never lie.

Expand your ring of confidence
by forging through your ring of fear.

There are things we are each afraid to do. Maybe it is to speak up in a loving way in our relationships for our desires and wants. Maybe it is that we are afraid to approach that man or woman and see if they would like to go out on a date. Maybe it is fear of asking your boss for that raise or promotion.

Whatever the fears are that hold you back, they are nothing more than an illusion made up of our own beliefs and memories. Once you begin to hunt down those fears and forge through them, you will see they were nothing more than **F**alse **E**vidence **A**ppearing **R**eal.

Hunt down those fears and face them.

Rain, sun, thunder and lightning are
all important to the balance of life,
just as joy, sadness, frustration and anger
are important to our balance in life.

We often think that some of our emotions are not
appropriate for us to feel. The truth is that they
are all appropriate to feel as long as we are
taking responsibility for them.

For us to feel and become aware of those emotions
and work through them is very important for
us to create balance in our lives.

When we are angry, frustrated or sad we need to look
within and see what is being "triggered" inside of us.
Those things that get touched usually have their roots
in our past and are being set off through something that
is currently happening. We can choose to look within
and see what is getting touched, rather than throwing
our anger onto the people around us.

If we learn to deal with these things that have gotten
triggered it can make our lives so very different.

Allow those emotions to come up and look within to
see what is getting touched in the moment. Then take
the time to share with those you love.

We fall in love, we fall out of love.
The truth is that when we are in love
we are open, honest, we share ourselves fully.

When we begin to close down, hide things,
or not share openly, we fall out of love.

If a couple sees all sides of each other, no secrets kept, and can love each other at that level, they will continue to remain close for as long as they keep up this level of intimacy.

It is when we begin to hold back and retreat, no longer sharing at a deep level, that love dies. When couples stop sharing, making each other important, being open and honest, then the feelings begin to wither. You are not falling out of love, you stopped showing up and risking with each other, the love is just buried under hidden feelings and words.

When we feel that we are no longer important in the relationship is when we begin to look elsewhere.

Yet when our eyes begin to wander it is a sign for us to look at where we are holding back in the relationship or where things that created the closeness are no longer happening. When we figure that out and share it with our partners we can begin to recreate the closeness. Often instead of sharing all this with our partners we think going outside the relationship will work best...it never does.

Courage is to be who I am whether someone is looking at me or I am looking at myself.

To be who I am alone or with others.

Often we will be one way when we are with others and another when we are alone. Integrity is when we are the same whether we are with others or alone. We hold the same values in both cases, we show up true to ourselves and our actions follow our words.

It takes true courage to be who we are in the face of others but even more so that we follow through when we are alone.

When you look into the mirror who do you see, a person of honor, honesty, integrity? Or someone different? What would you like to see when you look at yourself? When others see you? There is nothing more important than to be your word. When you are, your world will work very well and people will trust, honor and love you.

Be who you are, ask for what you want,
show all sides of yourself to the person
you want to be with, and if they stay,
they will stay forever.

*We often show our best side to those that we are
dating, in the hopes they will like us or love us.
When we spend our time trying to please the person
all the time and not being real we are setting up the
relationship to fail. Eventually you will tire of trying to
please them all the time and want to get back to being
yourself and having your needs met in the relationship.
When our needs are not being met we will find
ourselves finding fault with our partners and getting
angry. Yet we have set this up ourselves by only
showing what we thought that person wanted us to be.*

*If you want a relationship that is true and constant,
be who you are, show all sides of yourself to the
person you want to be with. Share what is going on
for you, ask for your needs to be met, find out about
what is going on for them and if the person can handle
the things you are showing them, they will stay forever.
If they cannot, then they will choose to leave.*

*You're better off being in a relationship with a person
that wants the real you than with someone you are
always trying to please. Be honest about your past,
show them your strengths as well as your weaknesses.
When you have nothing to hide and they are
still there, they will stay forever.*

*It is not about trusting the other person,
they will often let you down.
It is about trusting yourself to handle
whatever the other person does
and know that you are ok.*

We cannot control what others do or don't do. What we can control is what we do with what they say or do. We often put our trust in others and close our eyes hoping they will not let us down. Our job is to keep our eyes open, know that people are doing their best to get their needs met just like us and see when they are behaving in ways that are not in alignment with their words. Trust what a person does, not what they say.

Recognize the differences. Find out what love means to them and what being close means to them. We often have different meanings of things and yet do not take the time to find out what we each want. Take time to know if you are on the same page with the people you love.

Change is one of the miracles of life.
Be willing to surrender who you are
for who you can become.

As we let go of who we are,
we can embrace who we can become.
Yet change is scary, and we often want
to hold on to who we are rather than change.
Change takes courage and strength to let go
of what is and flow with what can happen.
What comes into our lives is something greater
when we flow with things.

Today just allow yourself to flow with
what life presents to you!

To create something different in your life,
expect to receive things differently.
Remember, the universe responds
purely to your expectation.

*We have conscious and unconscious expectations
and what we draw into our lives comes from those
expectations. Can you remember a time that you
wanted something and as you thought about it, life
began to bring things to you in order for you to have
that? Life will present you with what you are asking for.
Our unconscious expectations often carry more energy
and so those things will be brought to us first.*

*When someone or something comes into your life,
learn from it, use it to become stronger. Know that
everything you have, you have in some way called
to you in order to learn and grow from.*

*As you learn from it you leave room for the
next thing to come into your life.*

*Our biggest regrets in life are either
what we have done or not done.
The ones that truly haunt us are
either the things we have not done or
things we have done where we are
out of integrity with ourselves!*

As my friend was dying she continued to talk about the regrets she had in her life. Her regrets were around things she had done or not done in her life. As I began talking with others who were dying, I found that they too felt the same way.

The opportunities that they had missed, the things they had put off, either saying or doing, were what bothered them the most.

Take time to sit down and ask yourself, "What would I do if I only had one year, one month, one week or one day to live?"

Write out your bucket list today, the things you would like to see, do or create with those you love. You do not have to be dying to do this. Start creating those things today so there is no regret.

Sharing your dreams and burdens
allows you to get the support
you need in order to fly!
It allows you to be an inspiration
for those around you.

*Often we think we have to keep our struggles
to ourselves. How can you or those around you
learn if you are not sharing your struggle with them?
When we share the struggle we make room inside
ourselves for the answers to the struggle to come.
When we hold it in, there is no room for creativity
to find the answer to the struggle.*

*Sharing allows those around us to be inspired and
to see how to work through their own struggles as
well. I often think of what my children have shared
with me. My husband and I would often share with
them when we came up against obstacles. Sometimes
they came up with a way through the struggle we
were having. They have often said that it taught them
to see their way through their own struggles and
how to handle those times.*

*They learned that when they share their burdens,
they become lighter, and when they did not
share they became heavier.*

There are no accidents;
everything wonderful has lessons to it
and everything painful has lessons as well.
Sometimes we are too close to see
the gifts within the lessons.

I had often heard that there were no accidents, and today I can see that as true. Things happen to us that make us stronger or that bring us a piece to the puzzle of our lives. Everything happens for a reason and when we can let go of needing to know in that moment, we can see the opportunities in those packages much later.

As a young child I was sexually abused and in that abuse, as I healed, I found the amazing gifts that I received from that abuse. I learned to listen to others at a deep level, sometimes to what they were saying as well as what they were not saying verbally. Often their behavior said what their words could not.

I learned how to become very sensitive and aware to the things happening around me. When we step back and look at what gifts have come out of our pain we have a new respect for the pain that comes into our lives and how to learn from it. What gifts can you see in your life today that came from something you see as painful?

There are miracles
occurring around us all the time.
Those moments that can take your
breath away and leave you in awe.
Are you keeping your eyes open to see them?

*We can tend to get so wrapped up in
our lives that we miss those precious
moments that take our breath away.
Sometimes it is with people,
sometimes with places.*

*Stop and take the time to be present with
the people in your life that are inspiring,
who bring you to a place of awe.
Practice gratitude for the beauty
that is in your life and you
will see even more beauty.
Allow life to take your breath away
and leave you in awe.*

*We each have a purpose here on earth,
we each bring something unique to this world.
It is meant for us to live that purpose
in order to bring to life our gift.*

It is as though each one of us is a blade of grass
in the lawn of life. When one or more of those blades
are missing we begin to have bare spots in the lawn.
When your voice is not heard or you think
you have nothing to contribute, and don't speak
up or show up, then we all suffer.
Every team you are on suffers.
We miss out on the learning you bring
to all of us. Each one of us brings
something special to life. Our gift is
something we do naturally and for us it
would not seem to be unique
or special, but to others it is.
You are an important part of life.
Bring your uniqueness to those
of us in your life.
Share your gifts.

If you are telling yourself you can't,
then you won't!

*We find the people in our lives
to support what we believe.
If you continue to tell yourself you can't,
you will find the people to support
that belief and hold you back.*

*What do you want to create with your life?
What do you want your life to stand for?
Go out there and create those dreams!*

About the Author

Sue Paige is an internationally respected leader in the training and development field. With over 30 years of experience, Sue combines street smarts and real world experience with a straight talking approach to solving problems and creating extraordinary results, in order to inspire others to go further than they ever thought possible.

Sue is committed to creating a better world for families and children through the mission of Pathways to Successful Living Seminars, the company she and her late husband founded in 1984.

She has worked with business professionals, couples, college students, young adults and children alike to recognize the power of their own creative energies, and has mentored their success as they achieve their goals and dreams. Sue has an uncanny way of relating to people; it does not matter their age or profession, she gets right in there with each individual at their level.

Sue is a physical and sexual abuse survivor, has had multiple near death experiences, created an amazing love story and shared a passionate, immensely fulfilling marriage and career. Sue has found her four children to be her greatest teachers and the inspiration for much of the work she does today. Her greatest joy is time spent with her children and her four precious grandchildren.

To find out more about the Pathways to Successful Living Seminars, please visit the website at www.PathwaysSeminars.com.

Made in the USA
Monee, IL
29 April 2020

27724962R00066